SKYLIGHT

SKYLIGHT

ANTONY DI NARDO

RONSDALE

RONSDALE PRESS
3350 West 21st Avenue, Vancouver, B.C., Canada V6S 1G7
www.ronsdalepress.com

Typesetting: Julie Cochrane, in New Baskerville 11 pt on 13.5
Cover Design: Julie Cochrane
Paper: 70 lb. Husky (FSC) — 100% post-consumer waste, totally chlorine-free and acid-free

Ronsdale Press wishes to thank the following for their support of its publishing program: the Canada Council for the Arts, the Government of Canada through the Canada Book Fund, the British Columbia Arts Council, and the Province of British Columbia through the Book Publishing Tax Credit Program.

Library and Archives Canada Cataloguing in Publication

Di Nardo, Antony, 1949–, author
  Skylight / Antony Di Nardo. — First edition.

Poems.
Issued in print and electronic formats.
ISBN 978-1-55380-544-1 (softcover)
ISBN 978-1-55380-545-8 (ebook) / ISBN 978-1-55380-546-5 (pdf)

  I. Title.

PS8607.I535S59 2018   C811'.6   C2018-905514-6   C2018-905515-4

At Ronsdale Press we are committed to protecting the environment. To this end we are working with Canopy and printers to phase out our use of paper produced from ancient forests. This book is one step towards that goal.

Printed in Canada by Island Blue, Victoria, B.C.

to my sons,
Ariel and Aaron

—clouds,
like the inside of your head explained.
—JAMES TATE

I am drinking beer with yellow flowers
in underground sunlight
and you can see that I am a sensitive man.
—AL PURDY

CONTENTS

– May June July –

– Keep Frozen –

– Illuminations –

Skylight

Basquiat at the AGO had a painting repurposed
that worked itself into our everyday spaces.

On plates and vessels and parts of the sky
he boxed in the light so we could see it for ourselves.

I saw some words in it I thought I could use:
scarlet, rose, vermilion, shades of the trickster.

I saw my late uncle sit for a portrait.
Words in a bubble. Thoughts in a cloud.

I saw the intensity of knowing what we know
and from where it comes.

Artifice and invention on walls and windows.
Art lovers everywhere.

The gift shop was bright and spacious.
Articulate even. Art to pin on a chest.

As for the presence of anyone who might
read a poem, I couldn't say.

– Opus Erectus –

Autumn

Autumn sets up a tripod.
The trees stripped down.
Mountains where once there were none.

I walk ablaze with old romantics, Auden
rendering under heaven cause to be awed
by this dominant absence of leaves,

something entirely meant for me.
I'm sucked in by the barren beauty of the missing
and gone. A last minute lark in the branches,

here when everyone else has left,
sings a sorry jingle I know well.
Soil in the garden boxes, rotting,

cold and wet, dead and wishing for winter.
As for me it's the sun and its heat today,
first of November, that keeps me working,

hanging up leaves: ironic, neurotic,
forgetful, pressings and opinions,
written on the backs of these trees.

Remains

Reeds in the rushes, flutes in a quiver,
the last notes of a Grecian fall, a study in the art
of ruins. Sounds of the bent, broken,
and dun. Remains, in other words.

A triceratops, dead on its back, all bark
and bones, takes on a transparent lustre
off the morning light from the wedge of the moon.
Its bloated belly at the bottom of the marsh.

A distant relative, blue jay, comes to pay its respects,
has the jitters, perches,
preaches from the branches of the pulpit.
Skittish, the woods barely shield the unseen from view.

It's strange to be here at my Walden, benched, blanched
by the morning moon. If only you could see me,
between book and pencil, writing down the rest
of my story, my life on the flute, my days in Elysium.

The Lark

His eminence, the lark, is fond
of bonbons, finds them among dead leaves,
woodland draws, swollen bowers.

There's purpose to his hips, swung
in praise of articulation, the state of
the bosom, flight from the nest.

There's purpose to landing. Heaving
to suckle roots, naked
as a Borgia, the rock face of a slope

with its nose in the air, sniffing the air,
the pungent tart of hemlock.
The lark lives in its renaissance, a quick

study of soft feathers, velvets, silks,
brocades in the arms of the conifers,
an ancient family that rules. Its shelters

and stores add concupiscence to any garden,
woodland flare, to any poem that allows the lark
to wander in and out, unannounced.

The Hemlock

His most noble lord,
the hemlock,
says little.

His presence sufficient
to state the norms
of the phyla,
his Bach to the winds
when the horns
begin to play,
a case of intelligence
to add to the canon.

He's Mother
Nature's prince.
Mother Nature's
footprint
in every word
she writes, song
she sings.

A cappella
when the band
goes off to bed.

Portrait

Seven miles from here that's America.
The ridges, roadside stands,
old maples, have ripped
apart the clouds of imperfection.

And there it is. The sky
exposed. I puff and puff to let the demons out.
I love how they play *cache-cache*,
how they visit the elderly a-dying.

Four or five Americans agree
the world is round
and good and full of plenty.
How still they stand is enough for me

to get them right, their portrait
composed of distance, demons,
and four or five maples
by the side of the road.

I Write and Write

I write and write and nothing happens.

It's only rain, washing away in the pond.

Earlier, the thumbnail of a moon would not trade places
with the trees held in my hands.

The sun was beginning to rise but the moon stayed put.

Caught, I could tell, in the branches I kept sprouting.

– Fool Hen –

*Lines Written on the Occasion
a Spruce Grouse Came into the House*

Portrait of a Grouse

How to pick a drop
of pink without a brush?

Stitch an open wound
with just a beak?

She makes house calls.
Tears down walls.

She's blinded.
She's broke and winded.

She's in the room.
Thrumming through.

She's footloose, flight-lost.
Answers to *Fool Hen*.

A dust of dawn on feathers.
Autumn on her palette.

She's half the sun.
The other half

moonlight
bristling on her gown.

She's totally Morrisseau
about size and sorrow.

She's fingers trembling.
Fat thighs on the couch.

Leaves blend.
Browns patch.

She goes without,
comes within.

Paints a portrait of herself
entirely without wings.

No Room for a Grouse

That's no way for us
to be looking at her.

She's scared to death.
She's trapped and trembling.

Giants loom above her.

How many corners
to a wooden box?

She'll never know.

She'll never know
how light comes in the room.

Why woodland shadows blink.
How corners meet.

The mix of black and blue,
electric white.

She's no Pauline Johnson.
No Thunderbird. No master builder.

She'll never know
"Where Leaps the Ste. Marie."

She's in another world.

She rounds out the sky in her throat.

She doesn't see the forest
for the kiln-dried wood.

Trees that fell some time ago.
For a room that will never do.

This can be no place for her.
Where blood and timber contradict.

Where dead wood's boxed.
Contained.

She's fear and feathers all in one.

She's mortified.

She's minimized.

Best look away.

Ornithology

tells us
the tail gives her away.
She's *Falcipennis canadensis*.

Neither type nor genus,
nor name of species,
nor tree of life can protect her here.

She's built for spruce and pine,
not here.
Not this room.

She's made for bottom boughs,
burrs and branches,
winter rust, dead leaves.

Needles.
She's made for Birney
and Al Purdy,

Don McKay
in Sutton township
where feathers hide

by dim of dusk, din of fear,
fastened
to familiar ground.

She's broad shouldered
and barometer.
She's Ted Hughes.

She's wings-won't-lift.
Wants lift.
Wants wide,

wide berth.
She's what won't leave
without a flight plan.

Fool Hen

We've uncovered a plot to divide our world
from hers. A woven wire netted space, served
a purpose, debugged the room, moved the air.
Now there's a tear, a screen asunder, absence

in a severed line, the web that breached a boundary,
exposed our world to hers. The ordinary and mundane,
the daily acts of life, trees and such, all lined up
on the country road when I was turning right

then left for town. That day, across the border, post-
Thanksgiving, US eagles landed smug at every door,
holiday specialists on NPR. We love, as we all love
to live, our clever means of production. What with bread

and butter, eggs and cheese, how many ways to skin
a calf, stuff a bird, monetize the marketplace?
I come up Dyer Road, bag-heavy, park the Outback,
start all over. Fool Hen, de-clucked, clued-out, compass-

bent, flies right into our world and then into our arms.
Radio waves call like snow's been this way since time
began. Winter always black & white, black & white
on snowbound days. Whatever she may be doing

in this world, in either world, is not a question that I hear.
Nature captions all I need to know, my eyes this big
on where she sits balled up in a corner. Yet, somehow,
compassion for a bird like this has given me a set of wings.

What the Spruce Grouse Lost

The moon came out
with her latest disc,
the big sigh of the season.

A bird came flustered
in our house,
her sighs around the clock.

Such a breath of light upon the table.

Such a weight of feathers left behind.

Lady Grouse

You're bigger than your man
    you're bigger
    you're bigger

Your chest thrust forward
    your bosom
    a bulwark
    a double-breasted bastion

Hunter
    you stalk the berries
    pin the seeds
    seek the spruce

Headhunter
    you don't miss a thing
    your eyes like a hawk
    your eyes on the beak

Lady Hunter
    your nerves of steel
    you prey on fear
    on peril

    on men like me

Grammar for a Grouse

your predator
the goshawk
is a preposition—

most beautiful
of all parts
of speech—

a higher glyph
for the links
in the chain

the sky
a ligament
for its nest

connective tissue
in the mind
of a sentence

the ins and outs
of a life
in a case like yours

Fool Hen Sonnet

My lucky day, my feathered find, my kindred found,
now gone well beyond the woodland spawn
where once in fattened leaves you lived, hemlock
cones and needles in the ferns, the thick and lambent

burial ground of ample woodland maples, wetlands
winter-browned, pine nets lifting, bending,
marked with tamaracks. That's where you, Fool Hen,
lived in autumn leaves and lowland boughs

that tipped the ground beneath and in that place
you rested, nested, dug in nodes of wintry waste.
Like thoughts towed gently towards a skyward heave,
you're all the woodland grace I need.

Fool Hen Sits at Home

Toe- and fingernails grow at alarming rates.
There are two moons over the hill tonight.

Two moons in a book I read last night.
The crest on her head. The soft, unblinking eyes.

Her beak of bits and bone. Her claws. We make
a woollen space for feathers, wings, pine boughs

from the ground. Out of windows, glass and turmoil.
Clippings, lawn and leavings. Here,

in my head, she's a needle in the knitting.
Her backbone, pterodactyl.

Spruce Grouse Takes a Ride

I drove a bird deep into the woods.
We watched the pond fly by,
the snow withdraw,
the wind whipped into shape.
We listened to autumn hold its breath.
It took a thicker skin
to get there, a coat, for sure,
a fleece of feathers all buttoned-up.
I wore my winter tires.

I drove a bird into the woods today.
The trees were holding hands,
the mist around their heads a shawl,
a dip of draws and winding trails
nestled in a scant of scattered leaves:
no depth of field, no feigned perspective,
no trick of light to ease the flight
into a mixed deciduous north
New England state.

I drove the bird into the woods.
I sat behind the wheel
and put my wings in forward.
The bird was tasked with feathers,
I was asked to leave her world.
The clouds in common come from here,
a lesson in a pair of wings, and
like oxygen dissolves in parts per million
I drove and drove and disappeared.

Grouse Exit

Who let her in, we don't know.
How she let herself in, we don't know.

A box has built-in exits.
In her heart there's no way out.

The wobble and spin of the sun, the moon
make sense to her, but not this.

There's motherhood and then there's fear.
There's the dictum of the fittest.

But she can't get out.
Door is a concept she never cracked inside the nest.

We pick her up—it's physical—the heat
of an infant in our arms. We raise her. Carry her.

Take her as far as where the trees
become the sky.

And there she stays
long enough for us to leave.

– May June July –

Here on Earth

in the universe
> the universe
> of Hubble and Armstrong
> and Neil deGrasse Tyson

the only coordinates for
> the marsh marigold

are here on earth
> and here on earth
> the rhubarb the coltsfoot

a garden
> to raise
> > the seasons

Cowslip

the cowslip
          such a slight thing
leans into the slope of a draw
          a common flower
commonly in view
          as just another
bankside beauty
          that runs full tilt
towards oblivion

Woodland Violet

what woodland violet would want
       more
than woodland
rain
and rain
sun, yes
what we need
       but no more
           no more
than
that

Rose

imagine
given to naming
flowers
stones
the bones in a bag
bark on a tree
the pedigree
of dogs
darkness
the stars
one by one
illuminating
the names
given them
on a pair of lips
the tongue
lacquered
with a shade
of pink
we've named
rose

Lupine

one
frightened
lupine
(that's all it takes)
one
frightened
lupine
to bow our heads

Violets

look how lovely the violets
    the violets
        have a lovely voice
for a zephyr soft and *gentilissimo*
    una voce degli angeli

listen closely
to the dew
on their cheeks

Iris

the organizers behind the moon
                had principles
                        to govern by

the sign of the crab and water
                terrestrial
                        her gardens lunar

the iris purple as a moonlit night
                when sleep refuses
                        to come

her face the phases
                cheekbones high
                        certainly symmetrical

her eyes and shadows by design
                for how they saw themselves
                        reflected

Entangled

cancer
　　　　(there is no other word for it)
cancer
　　　can't kill
　　　　　the cherry
clematis
the crane's bill
　　　can't kill
the willow
　　　nor the side of the house
where sunlight
　　　props up
　　　　　the lily
the blight
and the ivy
　　　　　entangled

Leaves

a sheaf of sunlight for Spring
        a wing
and another
and another

until it comes to this
        leaves
deep deep
and green

The Creek

the chuckle of the creek
behind the house
    back bent in the rock
    rock bent back in its
coursing through
    bend by bend
    to the silt at the bottom
    of the pond
where it stows a basic element
    iron-cold
    iron-clad

Maple

an act of recovery
        the maple buds
an act of parliament
        the sap begins to run

The Great Green

I'm sorry, sir
your garden, sir, is in the final stages
it has three months to live

insensitive as we are to the fallen branch
the garden compensates

living things do die

a cell is banished

there's withering and there's wilt

I'm sorry, sir, you can't, sir
your brain is in the final stages
you have three months to live, sir

great green network   expanding universe
meadows growing the good wind blowing
we're surprised   the wiring
the great green brain to wane

I'm sorry, sir, yes you can, sir
feel that way
feel such beauty shouldn't lose its mind

a flower fades the garden wastes away
an image takes the place of what was left behind

a talking tree a talking tree
in the language of dead leaves

The Road

the road over-winters past
the gardens past
the climb past
the roadside woodruff
an accumulation of all
        that's come this way

then forks until
the waters swallow
       all that's gone away

Dawn

duckweed for the ducks
deadwood for the doorway

a pail of hemlock
              pinecones
for the gathering
          of the Fibonacci Association
              purveyors
          of the spiral

souls
          and suns and
                    swirls

brought to us at
          the breakneck speed
of dawn

Lace

(you're the whorl of the restive mind
    the spin
        and furl
of fingers curled
into the arms
    of a chair

the eye of a pistil
the lips of a stamen

fractal
    of Queen Anne's lace
        a shade less than tranquil
    a tad more than equal
        to the sum
of its physics)

you're like the house on a snail
    that spirals
        and seizes
    the trail
        she leaves behind
the snail
    bedazzled
        by the math
    on her back

Four O'clock

it is four o'clock and the four o'clock
    flower
opens its doors
    a yellow grin
    on its gate
yellow as once
    I remember
    Spring came late

Not Arrogance

after Jana Prikryl

not arrogance but coloured
not coloured but appropriated by the vessel of a garden
not bedded but rooted to the vehicle
                              of photosynthetic success
not success but greening
not green but coloured
and certainly not arrogance

Periwinkle

I had forgotten—how can I
or anyone remember everything—that
every living thing takes itself
so seriously except for members
of my *sapiens* species
who live this long to tell

a tadpole gets to be the frog only ever the one way
it always goes along the creek

I saw the periwinkle purpling down the bank

berserk

mid-afternoon

blue sky

the sun was shining

history was being made

Tall Trees

sturdy maple brother sister
birch
       the highlands of
the Appalachians

                comfort

even onto the tallest of trees
even as to how things are going
           between
                  two people

For Susan

contempt
       the big "C"
contaminates
          crushes
every black-eyed
Susan

condemns every cell
in a body of work

corrupts the daisy
in the good and curious

half a mind incomplete
chrysanthemums about to burst

half an organ insufficient
for the heart to bear

Foxgloves

endless pews
of hanging
heads
we call foxgloves
      supplicants
            more like it
hoodies
      begging
            always more
and more
of the morning
sun
as if they can't wait for later

Phlox

phlox be on earth
as it is in a 7-Eleven
plentiful and various
never rationed
cigs behind the counter
milk jugs and
amplitudes
the fecund
the ready and beware
all those who trespass
against the phlox

there will be phlox on earth

peace out

Dandelion

we smuggled beads from Arabia
hearts from the Qadisha
seeds in our pockets
the rootstalk of an impossible lemon

we took cuttings from the fig and the olive
the oleander and the flag of England

we took a shining to the sea

we smuggled out we smuggled in
we stowed away
we burrowed we borrowed we begged
    and we stole

but we never stood out
never stood taller than how we stand now
stalked across the lawn
    tooth of a lion
blade after blade after blade after blade

Picture

a trembling aspen
Puccini the cat
dead maple prone
to the side of the road
in a painting by a painter
who painted the picture of the photograph
I took at the window
overlooking the garden
one Sunday
May June July
opposite the wall
where it hangs

- Keep Frozen -

Yesterday at the Grange

Being here is just a way of not forgetting

1.

Words have a way with words,
of twisting the truthiness of things,
tweaking our resolve to face what we remember
with every blow to the head,
taking it fully in the mouth
where sometimes words prefer a friendship
with a metaphor,
the soft pedalling of a dead leaf falling
frozen in that moment's awe,
that moment of suspension
when the image calls a memory to itself.

2.

Yesterday I stepped on lines
by Brand and MacEwen, Acorn and Michaels,
memorable lines, images
stamped and frozen into the brick at the Grange,
head over heels with the poetry at my feet,
first day of autumn without a cloud, trees
in full disobedience, the city heat, Toronto,
eyelids on the face of the sun
wide open, just as I remembered.

The Crafte So Longe to Lerne

To see the forest for the trees

Poetry comes and goes like a doe and her fawn
might show up only briefly on the edge of the words

then leave you doubting what it was you've written,
the first flowers of spring or was that the river

going by? I'm a nature poet and it's in my nature
to commune with the dead. To talk to the quick.

I'm a record of the words I'm in. Of the phlox and
goldenrod, occasional flights of blue skies and clarity,

of words for rain and words for wet with not a chance
of a narrative to interfere with the forecast.

There are days when the muse appears unannounced
like the sudden flash of a white-tailed deer, like a leap

of faith to the other side of the riverbank.
I remember once foraging the woods for an image

and I forgot the word for syrup so I sipped on the sap
that dripped, dripped, from the tip of my pen

and I started to write.

"The crafte so longe to lerne" is a line from Chaucer.

Rilke or Sinclair

Metaphorically

Some poets like Sue Sinclair see flowers white
                              as an empty bed.

Rilke had this to say: "oh the two beds of my hands."

One way or another, light or dark, Rilke or Sinclair,
how each flower opens is beautiful
                    and beauty is most of all asleep.

"flowers white / as an empty bed": Sinclair's line comes from her book,
Heaven's Thieves.

Reading Eileen

*The accordion went on and on
until I could no longer hear it*

Reading Eileen
Myles
and listening
to NPR
the doors
shut
against December
the light
a composite
of rooftops
flashing
grades
of empty
sky
some slats
on the windows
open
for the light
to exit
and
there exists
an awareness
that leaks
between the two
of us
lingering for
so long
together
I know
you will return
even after

your brief
goodbye
was meaningless
I mean you're
too often
understated
or misunderstood
you'll forget
I asked
to buy us beer
and we've been out
of bread
since when
you left
the last time
you said goodbye
goodbye
you called it out
like that
from the door
but I was out
in the usual
way I'm usually
out of it
I mean
I was
reading
and I was
listening
to a recording
going on
and on
at the same time
I was
writing
you
this poem

For Don

Geopoetry in the Anthropocene

Among the rocks at sea
I read the poet *canadensis*
most likely to know the origins
of basalt, the whereabouts
of igneous, Prometheus, and
the metaphor that drives
Neptune's trident deeper.

His striations rise vertically,
deep core rust indents
the water's edge like rock
might draw the sea
into capillaries, like margins
mark the ragged right and
siphon Neolithic blood, fire-
form the knuckles for
this rugged eastern coast.

Black-fisted, black, black
as sun permits, flat-bottomed,
round of shoulders, form-fitted,
I sit among immortal rocks
and read McKay, Don
who knows a thing or two
of where the sea might
take a poem, or of basalt's song
sourced and quarried
for a poet's rock at dawn.

Rock Star

Objects are already sorted in the womb

A rock folds itself in two
turns into
the creek at the foot
of the bluff
carries the air
like anything else
that comes from the stars
also perceives itself from a distance
detached
maybe or perhaps
as far away as the mind of the poet
who takes the rock
and folds it into a sheet of writing

The rock screams surreal
the way writers do things
with a gang of words   take and take
until they make
something out of nothing
until they get
one on top of the other only to get off again

A rock isn't like that

It's one of those things that multiplies by dividing

Pointe-Claire

My sisters' DNA

Dozens of roads mismatch,
      crisscross, unleash the likely
final episodes of a suburban
      life around the table.

An in-law misspeaks, misdirects, channels
      the virtue of planetary stars and
alternate effects. A sister reads ingredients
      to put her child to sleep.

A heated oven. A candied house.
      Cardinals and strays.
Three sisters, chatty, charming, galvanized,
      familiar with the spell:

Renew, repeat, and reassert
      the potion in our DNA.

Deer Whistles

Bande dessinée

Ducks and geese and the woman with the red dress
had themselves quite a winter, but the geese especially,
dipping their brains into the fat of the lake,
ass-end up, foraging for shit beneath their feet.

A boat comes in full harbour, docking between piers.
I've seen this before, the boat, the landing, a bright brilliant
blue afternoon sky, saw it in a movie, in a book, a painting
I stood against for the longest years when I was young.

So here they come again, refugees from the past on a ferry,
on a farm, like blades of grass in the wind screaming
"I've been on the best ride ever!" Young bodies flung
to shore and solidly embracing satisfaction.

I made a picture of it, I mean I sketched it in my notebook,
the story sketching itself with the same words I used
to tell of a boat slowly coming into harbour to dock behind
the watercolour of a lighthouse that I once punctuated

with lodgings on the lakeshore, camouflaged as laundry
on the line. I remember Cobourg, the King George Inn,
deer whistles that day as a first line of defence,
veterans with a working knowledge of Morse code.

Caliban Collects His Thoughts

*The sea and the mirror and something
from another poet*

That woman in the black strapless dress,
white star-studded cap, black top,
black car, is adjusting herself in increments of gradually
fitting in to the corn-high waves, a walk along the pier

suited to where the lakeshore will be lapping at her feet.
In a world of windows everyone looks out.
Even seagulls aren't ashamed to drip their scat
on banks below, squirrelly black

dogs on leashes in semi-democratic parks the same.
A lawyer who steps into a black Cadillac
and weaves out of her parking spot
is a rescue breed with the maw of a clenched fist.

Her cargo ship, I remember, was the recently divorced
and dead husband found floundering in the murky waters
of Corner Creek, headlines
attended to by beaks and brains and mismatched claws,

familiar smells in degrees of rotting flesh.
A smile on her face finds a seat in the upper colonies
and she turns her dead husband's ashes into prayer beads.
She's a crone on Sundays.

Her buttons are bone.
It is in a dark memory I most often see her
cutting heads off the fish, frightening gulls
with her one good eye.

So she fed me for years, my mother
who predicted the new world ways
in a brave new world. Yes, I remember the journey off
the island some good god shook out from the sky.

You know, I haven't aged for centuries, yet
I'm still learning to land on my own two feet,
remember favourite colours, keep elbows off the table,
hands to myself.

Scarlet, Rose, and Vermilion

At home in the heart of the mountains

I must leave Ottawa as soon as I can.
My pen is spent.

My thoughts on order and disorder
are confused and changing as I speak.

I'm inviting myself to the ball.
The ball that begins at midnight.

Why am I reluctant to be one with my shoes?
Or stand for too long in front of the US embassy?

It's embarrassing how I put two and two together.
Now I'm back.

The flannel of Fall and colours that come with it
catch up to me. I'm a cog in the cycle.

Everywhere else vast regions of mediocrity
bombard the senses.

But in the mountains they get lost
in the importance I place on scarlet, rose, and vermilion.

Hard Rain

I am sentimental

      I cry at the death of sailors, babies, LGBTQs,
      mothers, sisters, daughters.
      I cry at the sight of refugees.

I loved communism:
      I cried at its death. Castro and Cuba.

I loved the Beatles, their message, the bookstore on Queen.
I pick and choose my shoes.
My menus, the daily news.

I am very sentimental:
      I miss moments of nostalgia, I pine for
      my mother's Renoirs, her truly meaningful
      and melancholic memoirs.

I miss nostalgia. Rita and the rain.
Baudelaire. Nelligan. Saint-Denys Garneau
      on the steps of Montréal.
The very best of Pauline Johnson who wrote
      What dream you in the night-time
      When you whisper to the moon?
I miss those years they wrote about me long before
      I was ever born.

I miss my thesis, my dress code:
      the years at Sherbrooke and McGill.
The years I've put to rest.

I miss remembering testaments, interiors, retrospects.

I miss the shrill of something new.
    The ozone of experience.

But I am sentimental:
    And so I leave nothing behind.

Lilium canadense

A garden in the classical style

Forage and Main
Backpack and Medicine Man
Paddle and Grassy Narrows

Hike and Hinterland
Badlands and Midland
Shield and Fancy Goose

Attawapiskat
Fifth and Three Rivers
Bear and Barren Plains

College and Rain
Mainway and Runway
Redrock and Glare

Food Court

Subterranean home-cooked blues

The bees are faked.

A virtual buzz instills the air with an air of virtuosity.

It doesn't get more real than this.

The flora's just as duped.

Shades of neon downtown pink.

Sprays of manufactured lady's slippers, lupines, hair perfume.

The din of pink.

Glazed to wash away the gritty bits that stick.

The birds are faked; the ferns are fake.

And other words for song.

Here, where the animal in the belly learns to growl.

Where the benches are eco-friendly recycled imitation
     polymers, neo-outdoor revivalist by decree.

Here, where players known as patrons sit.

Where words imitate each other.

The trees in harmony harmonize with artificial casts of lighting
filtered through scrubbed acrylic planes of faux
transparence in long unbreakable chains of molecules.

Indoors.

Climate controlled.

With non-reactive plastic claws, knives and forks.

Prosthetic limbs poised on mannequins dressed in
subterranean gear.

Where headlines on the screens materialize unrealized.

Neutralized to emulate a woodlot in a concrete meadow.

Where I'm in line for bottled water.

Where the creek is dead.

Whitevale, Ontario

Parting is the song of the sweet, sweet sparrow

The sound of peepers, frogs at the mouth of the marsh,
redwings at roost, the light-conferring mind of a naturalist
at each door, the linden and the walnut glistening,
the rains gone, voices piping, green molecules rising
in the air.

The sun's never too old for this: tenderly it touches you
and should you resist, the gardens, backyard bird calls,
ample and exhaustive, answer for you.

If you sit or stand or step on any porch in town and listen,
some story will come to you, some playground of open sky
and airships groaning, distant mowers, funerals and
hallowed eves, Sunday strings boxed in icons of stained
glass, book sales by Don, chamomile and festivals that
peak in spring.

And those are just some of the things that will come to
you and keep you from ever leaving again.

Some Trees

A poem lovely as a tree

Some trees, like Ashbery's, sit on a shelf.
These are amazing: project an air of size,
stature, dimension. Even without shadows
they corner the limits of the sky.

You turn on a light in a room and a tree
has leaves, the chair a woodland back,
the table a little river. If birds came to live here
their nests would make a bed for two.

Some trees get hungry and talk to each other.
They order in, lick their fingers, lean in closer,
suck on the rays of the sun that might disintegrate
before they put a bark around it.

Some trees can fit inside your pocket
and improve upon the deliciousness of a murder
mystery at the lake. Some connect to other
powers: their branches touching, caressing,

holding hands, alive down to the very fibre
of their roots. Some trees are familiar. Live always
in one place. If they move they're reincarnated
as pulp and paper. These live alone, find

fame in the minds of others, like Kilmer's
tree, a word so lovely it evoked an entire forest
on the page. Some don't. Are clear-cut, chipped
and hauled to the pits, razed to make way

for the 407, Cornell, places with names like that.
Some trees get high as Mount Pinacle,
needles for their eyes to pierce every bit of light
so they stay green year round.

Some trees are older than you think.
They grow immeasurably even after they die.
They call themselves granddad, grandma,
help us heal. Some trees begin at six

and don't get home until five. Some change
colour: crimson, vermilion, scarlet, rose.
Some trees are ancestral, Devonian,
travel the world in paper airplanes.

Little bark boats. For some it's in their blood
to bleed. Some acquire a taste for touching
themselves, fondling the pink bits of their trunk.
Some grow in multiples of two.

Some trees like to hear new ideas and feed
on matter found in the wind, on fresh propositions
for lengthening their shadows. Some are like no other.
They seek the moon, stay up late, party,

shed their leaves, come home bent
and fall into a trance until spring, their memory
of the night before completely gone.
Some trees begin where others end.

"These are amazing" is taken from Ashbery's poem of the same name.
"A poem lovely as a tree" is from Joyce Kilmer's "Trees."

Woodworking

How many trees to make a forest?

I think of furniture as Swedish or French.
The rocking horse English.
The cabinet green.

I think of leaves as starting from scratch.
Trees at the brink of the next.

I think of furnished rooms in Baie-d'Urfé, Shawinigan,
St. Jacobs, Ontario.

I think of trees as furnishings and sublime.
Sturdy, reclining, robust, and on sale.
Reduced for clearance.

I think of inside and out.

I think of the first woman on the moon,
by the lake, by the bench.
The first to have a plate of greens.

A fish in a bowl. A tabletop.

I think of sitting down with her, of setting a place.

I think of roof and chair.

Of furniture as flat.

Solarium

Sky light and the physics of heat

You, full Sun, can coax infinity from above
        the trees and coat each palm translucent.
You can turn the current on. Single out the leaves,
        banana and green.

In your heat, torpid and drawn, happiness
        doesn't need anyone to walk the shores
or hear your voice—you're already filled to the brim
        and sunny as it could get.

Bodies belong to the ocean, like the mind
        of Kush and Tony belong to you,
hot, Hellenic, your gravitational wizardry
        on the trampoline of the newly-minted space/

time continuum calculated, imitated, rendered
        down to shape and size, painted, modelled,
picked at for some po-mo analytical aesthetic
        —and me basking in your

greatest hit, "Heat, Heat, Heat,"
        the azure sky, tropic and dreamy—
while Happiness walks the beach, picks up on
        the slap, slap, slap of waves

that are the same as singing
        I am ocean, I am ocean, you,
full Sun, pouring out your heart
        in blues and indigos,

aquamarines,
       and that special turquoise mid-day light
with never a shadow, never a shadow,
       only that of the moon when you leave.

On Three Paintings by Patychuk

You're on earth. There's no cure for that.

The room she occupies does the heavy lifting
in her work up on my walls, gold
the colour of wheat, a prairie waving frozen

to a Rocky, her waterworks breathing in
the white spruce from the couch, rivers thinned
to carry off the bones of the Indigenous dead;

in another, gold is tarnished but brilliant,
explosive for the roots becoming still-standing trees
you can climb into a cool blue sky, an open window

instead of a single house to bother with, an abstract
to soften edges like Beckett did when he looked Death
in the eye, hers veiled and obstinate, a green sensation.

"You're on earth. There's no cure for that" is by Samuel Beckett.

- Illuminations -

Le nuage

The figure reclining in the cloud that I snapped with
my phone today looked like it was by Georgia O'Keeffe,
painted during an early period when she often turned
to the sky to see what time it was, the image, a copy of
her *White Pansy* from 1927, stark yet softly petalled,
about which a poet might say that it's a photo of the
dead where the many-layered soul has left the body and
floated up into the heavens, whereupon she sees it today
as a larger-than-life reproduction slowly moving north,
northwest and occupying but a corner of the vast blue
canvas, which, wherever she looks, appears empty and
blank as if it has yet to absorb another soul or reveal
what time of day it is.

Chanson

I resisted the wild winds of winter for as long as I
could. All afternoon they came at me like fists over
the mountain. I couldn't write a word. I lost the
first round, beaten into a corner, silenced by the
beating I took. But when the sun went down, I
willed the wind to leave and I turned my back to
it, the terrible wind defeated at last. Darkness fell.
My victory so fired up the cells of my being I could
see well enough to turn on the overhead light and
sing the praises of passive resistance.

Petite méditation

The lives of the many empty out of rooms and
doorways topped with icing from the clouds,
azure blue with a deeper sense of tranquil that
gives the coast in this part of the world its name
and throughout the south a belt of snow-capped
peaks buckled far above the coast heightens the
solitude that looks down on red-tiled roofs,
cypress spears and crowning pines interrupting
the soft margins of this village, old and lithic,
rock walls perched on knuckles, footfalls
cloistered by its borders—a koan that sums up
how where one begins another ends—and, in
the distance, valleys I will never reach fall deep
into the sea as mountains crest at the peak of
noon when the bells of the nearby town hall
ring me back to Earth.

La terre est bleue comme une orange

wrote Paul Éluard, without any further explanation.
I think it's because the orange tree is green and so
is the lemon, both growing side by side in a garden,
the garden but a morsel taken from the mountain,
which, like any mountain, was released from the
rock, the ancient rock where Earth first gets its start
and, if seen from the distant sway of the moon, is
blue as the orange that rolled to the ground.

Le vent

However hard you try, you can't talk sense into a
wind that howls and blows and whistles and groans,
that never grows on you and won't hear a thing you
have to say, a voice louder than Wagner's on Radio
Classique, bigger and wilder than Rimbaud as it sits
on the roof and rattles and shakes every cliché you
can think of even as the wind takes your child into
the woods on the great green maw of its jaws and
flings her so far from you, you can't call her name,
your voice like the air itself that she'll never hear,
one wind whipping into another, fierce and fearless,
because it won't sit still for a second, and should you
find yourself in the crow's nest, mid-career, before
you can change your mind, the wind blows your ship
away, blows off the top of your head, makes your
teeth rattle, the windows rattle, reminds you that it
can see right through you, this wind that will take
your soul, leave you breathless, as it comes up from
behind the mountains to thoroughly confound you,
and, while this may be just a detail, this wild wild
wind that blows so unforgivingly doesn't know a
thing about you; it can't begin to describe the
terrible thoughts that have possessed you.

L'arbre

She said sit here next to me and I'll watch you paint
a poem of that persimmon tree there by the wall,
the fruit left hanging through the winter, the sun
brilliant today like a golden apple polished and bred
for sweetness, its long-lasting flavours persisting far
into the next season, unlike these persimmons, now
shrivelled, shrunken and unpicked, no one to
pucker their lips to the sweet juices that might ooze
from them when the skin gives way and the taste of
sunlight bursts into your mouth, wet and sensuous,
with you sitting here next to me.

La nuit

In winter, a town I know grows quiet at ten or
eleven, darkness profound, serving its purpose to
keep most people indoors, only a few of them out
in the wilderness of the local streets, their little
dogs on a leash, the bigger ones off, walking along
the side of the road where the grass has thinned
and the shrubs are torn, the hard dirt scratched
and scolded by both fresh and dried-out feces, a
familiar collection of sizes and shapes, shit that
dogs have distributed up and down the filthy
banks that flank the sidewalk where men, mostly,
at this hour walk their dogs and patiently wait for
them to mark their course, eliminate the body's
waste, before they bring them back into their
homes to empty bowls and scratch them in that
special place just behind the ears.

Les violettes

The flower vendor is a burly man, he's brusque
and bold, has his price and won't be budged,
his violets bunched in tiny packets, leggy stems
cupped in kitchen foil, the petals like fastened
dabs of purple eyelids, a palette soft and reticent
about the history of the woodland meadow where
they were picked that morning for the vendor who
carries them in a shallow wicker basket, his fingers
thick and bruised make a fist around each bunch
as he picks them from the fold. The rain has
stopped and now the cobblestones are slick and
glassy beneath the arch that fascinates how a
ruddy mountain man and the tender faces of his
violets merge in the mirrors puddling at our feet.

Le voyage

Some with wings, some wasted with wonderment,
one with someone else, the headiness of unflagging
love and happiness, existential miniseries that
qualify one's relevance, the foaming at the mouth
as people mince their words and say what they
don't mean, what they don't know, say what they
don't want, where they won't go, busy making plans
to leave themselves behind.

I know the minds of men and women are crowded
with dreams that are meant to escape the long
drought of eternity without so much as a backward
glance. They hold their breath, they count the stars,
they practice transcendental techniques to calm
their ghosts or disappear altogether, breathe against
the glass to hide their faces. They ride, they fly, they
polarize, they climb a peak, they medicate, trade
places, drink to feel something else about
themselves. I know they do. I do it myself.

YUL

A mother loves an airplane ride as much as her
child takes her back home to her family made
up of a table and chairs in a kitchen, a French-
Canadian home-cooked meal, a paycheque and a
barbecue in the summer with the weather far from
winter and far from what she imagined life on her
own if she had never left home at seventeen.

Le temps bleu

It isn't the same thing to say *ce n'est plus le même temps*
when what you mean is that it's late, the industry of
the vast blue sky meant to show us how time and not
the weather moves the seasons and its moods fallen
upon us with our many insecurities pertaining to
hurricane winds and greying clouds, that the sea off
in the distance is indifferent and altogether silent
when we see our features reflected in its multitude
of faces, the sea black and blue and sometimes
whitecaps, wintry waves surmounting all the colours
we've been given for the passing of time.

Terrible

The way weather rules the day, the first click of
the mouse, the mix of offence and defence on a
football pitch, black and grey, north and sun, a
clump of clouds, the stingy sky, a shadow wrapped
around a sixty square kilometre arbitrary patch
of planet (when I can see that far) flat as the eye
deigns to perceive the great design of nature,
torture of a cold and runny nose and paper
hankies, wings fluttering as the wind picks up,
then it rains, then there's snow and visibility the
next thing to let go when I shut my eyes and feel
the weather slashing at my face only to say it's an
article of faith to know that it can only get worse
before it gets better.

&

the village songbird, a direct descendant of
Baudelaire & Rimbaud, his village voice an
ampersand of song & gossip on the wire, comes
on at six, maybe five, either way long before
sunrise fries an egg, the light of morning expected
to be soft & runny, ratified as usual by birdsong

& the songbird sings his heart out, an a cappella aria
that fills the first of daylight, its light borrowed from
the midnight moon, so all the others might sleep a
little longer before attending to the business of the
nest, the poet adding to his repertoire, dawn about
to burst out from the rest.

Autoportrait

Brief of rain, a multiplex of syllables splattered on
the bedroom skylight, drumming fingers that I might
importune the rolling thunder, tune the air so
darkness can't tell where it's coming from.

Once I ran down a mountain racing the setting sun
to reach the valley before darkness fell and when I
looked to see what trail I left behind, the mountain
had completely vanished and I could barely discern
from where it was that I began.

Once I fiddled with the keys to my door like I had
symbols in my hand to find some other way out of
the rain, which I couldn't without the key that held
the reason I needed to let me in.

It is possible in parts of this country to climb the
highest peak in order to snag a passing cloud and
paste it, if you wish, in a notebook or a painting, or
in any self-portrait that otherwise seems incomplete
without it.

SKYLIGHT

I don't know the French word for it but
it's a four-sided box with a fifth side left
up to the imagination to draw light from
the sun that, from where I sit, cannot be
seen, the incandescent light of sky well
above my head and far from where I
strike a pose towards sleep, reading a line
of monkey poetry by Julie Bruck whose
book I hold comfortably between my
hands and, intended for a pair of human
eyes to see, brightens the two hemispheres
of the brain like glass filtering the light of
sky which I find difficult to resist when
written to resemble a column of words
justified to contain a poem illuminating
the right side of the page and little else.

"monkey poetry": this phrase is found in Julie Bruck's *Monkey Ranch.*

NOTES

These poems first appeared in the following publications, and I am grateful to their editors for allowing their appearance in this volume:

"Opus Erectus" in *Grain*.

"Ornithology" in *Tupelo Quarterly*.

"May June July" was winner of the Gwendolyn MacEwen Poetry Competition for Best Suite of Poems 2017, first published in *Exile Literary Quarterly* and nominated for a National Magazine Award. This poem is for Susan Briscoe.

"Food Court" in *Vallum*.

"Solarium" and "For Don" in *The Fiddlehead*.

"Some Trees" in The League of Canadian Poets' anthology, *Heartwood: Poems for the Love of Trees*.

ACKNOWLEDGEMENTS

I would like to thank Ann, first and foremost, for her sensitivity and keen eye as an artist and gardener. Her appreciation of light, from all its sources, has often informed and grounded my work. To my sons, Ariel and Aaron, I owe all the gratitude in the world for their unvarnished love and encouragement. And I am very much indebted to the following people: my publisher, Ron Hatch, whose faith in my work made this book possible; Steve McOrmond and Brian Bartlett for their generous feedback on the manuscript; my readers in friendship, who continue to tolerate my lyrical whims; Wendy Snowden and Ole Hoyer of North Vancouver, who have always encouraged excellence in capturing light; and to the people of Patnem Beach who provided the masala chai both at the start of this book and in its final revisions. Namaste.

ABOUT THE AUTHOR

Antony Di Nardo was born in Montreal and obtained a post-graduate degree in English from the University of Toronto. His writing career began as a journalist, publishing and editing a weekly newspaper in northwestern Ontario, and contributing poetry to the first issues of *The Squatchberry Journal*. Recent work has been translated into both French and Italian and has been anthologized in several collections of poetry and non-fiction. His first book, *Alien, Correspondent*, was shortlisted for the Acorn-Plantos Award for People's Poetry, and he has been shortlisted for *The Malahat Review*'s Long Poem contest. In 2017, he won *Exile*'s Gwendolyn MacEwen Prize for Best Suite of Poems. He now divides his time between Sutton, Quebec, and Cobourg, Ontario.